I Grew Up On A Farm

Written by Alan K. Lewis
Illustrated by Bob Fletcher

Published by Moo Press, Inc.
Warwick, New York

The text of this book is set in

16 point Comic Sans, with

headings in Chalk

and map text in Kids font.

Cover art by Bob Fletcher.

The illustrations are done in

graphite and pastels.

BVG 10 9 8 7 6 5 4 3

Published by Moo Press, Warwick, NY. An imprint of Keene Publishing.

For information on permission to reproduce, or about this and other Moo Press titles,

please e-mail info@moopress.com or write to Moo Press, PO Box 54, Warwick, NY 10990.

To order copies of this book, visit your local bookstore, or see our Web site at www.moopress.com.

Second grade reader shown on page 27 is from pages 60-61 of *My Word Book* by Frederick S. Breed

and Don C. Rogers; copyright 1954 by Lyons and Carnahan Publishers.

For more information on farming in the USA, see the list of Web sites at the end of this book. Many

thanks to historian Elaine Flynn for the tour of Slate Hill Schoolhouse, pictured on page 27.

And to Margaret Bennett for her skilled photo restoration services.

Library of Congress Cataloging-in-Publication Data

Lewis, Alan K.

I grew up on a farm / written by Alan K. Lewis ; illustrated by Bob Fletcher.— 1st ed.

p. cm.

Summary: A man remembers his childhood on a farm, including all the wonderful things that he,

his brother, family, and friends did at different times of the year.

ISBN-13: 978-0-9766805-2-9 (hardback : alk. paper)

ISBN-10: 0-9766805-2-1 (hardback : alk. paper) [1. Farm life—Fiction.] I. Fletcher, Robert A., 1931- ill. II. Title.

PZ7.L58457Iag 2005

[E]—dc22   2005018959

Proudly created, printed, and published

in the United States of America.

This book is dedicated to my dad, Lester Lewis, a city boy who followed his dream to become a farmer. He taught me to fish, to love nature, and to follow my dreams.

—A.L.

Dedicated to American family farming—past, present, and future.

—B.F.

Acknowledgments

I would like to thank my family for all their support and all of the people who said this project was a good idea. Many thanks to Wendy for the original sketches, Judy and Mary Margaret for all your advice, and to all the farmers out there in this great country of ours who put food on our tables. —A.L.

I must recognize my God-given gift of being able to create artwork through drawings and paintings. Thank you author Alan Lewis and Publisher Diane Tinney for allowing me the privilege of joining you on this book project—a worthy and wonderful experience. —B.F.

I grew up on a farm in a rural area not far from here. The farm is gone now, but I can still remember exactly what it looked like.

Old Calvin

I remember my dad telling me he went to college to learn how to become a good farmer. He studied how to plant and harvest crops and take care of animals.

The students practiced on the farm and in the fields of the college. One time, a herd of cows got into the cornfield. The cows ate all of the sweet corn just before it was going to be picked!

Soon after my dad graduated, he and Mom married. They bought this farm, and our life on a farm began.

My dad loved his truck. He hauled all the animal feed from town to the farm on his truck. He stored the feed in the big red chicken barn.

When I was twelve, my dad taught me how to drive the truck. I remember feeling so grown-up. Driving all over the farm was exciting. I tried to go slowly, and be careful, but one time I drove right into a haystack!

6

We raised chickens, pigs, cows, turkeys, ducks, and geese on the farm. Every day I woke up early and did my chores. One of my jobs was to carry the heavy pails of slop for the pigs.

We took care of the chickens, feeding them grain and water daily. In return, they laid many eggs that we sold. That's how we made a living—growing food for other people.

I had to gather eggs from the nests. The chickens didn't like that, and they pecked at my hand.

We sold dozens of eggs every week from our roadside stand. People would always ask me, "Are those eggs fresh?" I would say, "They are fresh from the chickens."

We sold to bungalow colonies and advertised in the newspaper. People drove from far away to buy fresh eggs, chickens, and vegetables from us.

When our chores were done, the farm became our playground.

Hay Field

Dig for Arrow Heads

Fossil Rock

Garden

The Spring

Best Fishing spot

Hide here

My cousins from the city visited often. They loved all the things we did on the farm. On hot summer days we ran through the fields, chasing ducks and chickens. We had contests to see how many grasshoppers and crickets we could catch.

My dad would take us for a ride in the back of
the truck. We rode all over the farm. It was a bumpy
ride through the hayfields, and we had to hold on
tight!

At night, we slept in tents under the stars. Our favorite nighttime games were playing flashlight tag and catching fireflies in jars to watch them light up.

Way past our bedtime, we finally drifted off to sleep listening to the katydids in the trees and the croaking of the bullfrogs in the pond.

We had six dogs on our farm, and cats everywhere! There were always plenty of puppies and kittens to play with in the summer.

One of our dogs was an Airedale named Sandy. She loved to sit with my brother and me in the cool shade of a maple tree near the pond. That dog followed us everywhere!

I fished almost every day in the summer. My cousins would fish with me. Along with fish, we caught salamanders, snakes, turtles, and frogs.

My brother and I caught the biggest snake in
the pond. After scaring the girls with it, we let it go.

I had a pet squirrel named Nutsy.
My cousins would laugh when he climbed
on my head.

Once, my dad got the tire of our Farmall tractor caught in a hole. The tractor flipped up and popped a wheelie! Luckily, no one was hurt.

On Sunday afternoons in the summer, my family would have picnics on the back lawn under the big maple trees.

At the big Labor Day picnic we ate barbecued chicken and corn on the cob from the vegetable garden.

Soon it was time to go back to school. When we
got home, we did our homework and then played hide-
and-seek in the big red barn.

Fall was a good time for riding horses. We rode horses all the time. When we were little, Mom and Dad would take us for a ride on their horses, Pokey and Bucky.

When I was older, I rode my own horse, Stormy. We named him Stormy because he was born in a field in the middle of a storm.

Galloping up the road was fun and a little scary because Stormy was so big and so fast. I always made time to ride him when my chores were done.

In the winter we went sledding on the big hill above the pond. We packed the snow down to make a slick run for our sleds. Then we raced down the hill and across the pond.

When our friends came over, we would build snowmen, throw snow balls, and ice-skate on the pond.

I loved winter on our farm. After sledding,
skating, and building snowmen, my mom made yummy
hot chocolate to warm us up.

The school bus picked us up in front of our house and took us to our school. The bus driver taught us to sing "The Wheels on the Bus" and "On Top of Spaghetti."

Our schoolhouse had only three rooms and three teachers. First and second grades were together in one room, third and fourth grades in another room, and fifth and sixth grades in the last room.

Here's what a typical classroom looked like back then. I remember how hard it was to keep the inside of the desk neat. By the end of the school year my desk was packed full of papers, broken crayons, artwork, and nubby little pencils.

My second grade reader looked like this. We would practice our letters and learn new words. I especially liked the stories about animals.

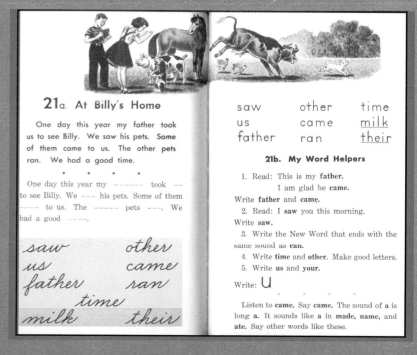

21a. At Billy's Home

One day this year my father took us to see Billy. We saw his pets. Some of them came to us. The other pets ran. We had a good time.

• • • • •

One day this year my ———— took —— to see Billy. We ——— his pets. Some of them ————— to us. The ————— pets ———. We had a good ————.

saw   other   time
us   came   milk
father   ran   their

21b. My Word Helpers

1. Read: This is my **father**.
   I am glad he **came**.
   Write **father** and **came**.
2. Read: I **saw** you this morning.
   Write **saw**.
3. Write the New Word that ends with the same sound as **can**.
4. Write **time** and **other**. Make good letters.
5. Write **us** and **your**.

Write: U

Listen to **came**. Say **came**. The sound of **a** is long **a**. It sounds like **a** in **made**, **name**, and **ate**. Say other words like these.

Growing up on a farm was fun for my brother and me, but it was hard work for my parents. Although they worked from sunup to sundown, they always made time for us at the end of the day.

Dad used to say that the best things he grew on his farm were his kids.

At the end of the day, after our baths, my dad, my brother, and I would read books and share stories about our day.

Then it was time to go to bed and dream of adventures to come.

Today...

Photo credit Sara Lewis.

The farmhouse still stands and has been modernized inside and out. The red barn is gone, and the green barn has been turned into a kennel with an office. Over the years, the trees have grown and the pond has dwindled to a stream.

Although I didn't go into farming, I never lost the love of growing things. An avid gardener and landscaper, I have a small greenhouse where I grow flowers and vegetables from seed, and then plant them in my yard every summer.

Sometimes I drive past where the old farm stood more than fifty years ago and relive the memories of my wonderful childhood days.

I am now an educator working in a modern school about a mile away from the old family farm site and my old schoolhouse. I enjoy helping students and teachers grow. I guess in many ways, I have followed in my father's footsteps, although I haven't had a tractor pop a wheelie on me yet!

Glossary

Airedale—a large terrier dog with a rough, black-and-tan coat

bungalow colonies—a group of small cabins in the country where people, usually from the city, come to stay for the summer

coop—a small pen or building for housing poultry

grain—small, dry seedlike fruit produced by cereal grasses (e.g. oats, wheat, barley, corn)

harvest—to gather in crops

katydid—a large green American long-horned grasshopper that makes a shrill sound

poultry—domestic fowl such as chickens, ducks, turkeys, and other birds kept for their eggs or meat

rural area—a place in the country

salamander—a cold-blooded animal shaped like a lizard

slop—a pig food made from grain, water, and pieces of vegetables

Learn More About Farming

Your school library and public library are good resources for you to learn more about rural life and farming. Just in case you can't get to the library, here are some Web sites that I've found useful. Many have kid-friendly pages with activities. Be sure to visit my Web site at www.IGrewUpOnAFarm.com too!

www.usda.gov
United States Department of Agriculture Web site. Everything from farms to nutrition.

www.nass.usda.gov/ny/
The New York Field Office for agricultural facts and figures. Great kids page.

www.agmkt.state.ny.us
New York State Department of Agriculture & Markets.

www.4husa.org
The United States 4-H Web site. Has links to local and international programs.

www.feathersite.com/Poultry/BRKPoultryPage.html
Terrific pictures and information about many different kinds of chickens and other fowl.

www.ffa.org
National Web site for Future Farmers of America news, activities, and education resources.

www.farmnet.osu.edu/links/kids.html
Hosted by the Ohio State University, provides links, activities, facts, and figures for kids.

www.IGrewUpOnAFarm.com
Official Web site for this book. Includes activities for students, lesson plans for teachers, and family fun for everyone!